D0450027

STARTING
TODAY

A JOURNAL OF

INTENTION AND CHANGE

CHRONICLE BOOKS

ISBN 978-1-4521-0936-7

Printed in China

Designed by Alexandra Styc

10 9 8

Chronicle Books LLC
680 Second Street
San Francisco, California 94107

www.chroniclebooks.com

INTRODUCTION

IN THE JOURNEY THROUGH LIFE, there are two approaches you can take. The first is the backseat approach, accepting the first thing life puts in your path and making do. While this way certainly reduces the stress of decision-making, the final outcome is rarely one of fulfillment. Then there's the second approach: living a life filled with intention. This way involves opening your eyes to your true needs and desires and acting on them.

Perhaps the biggest roadblock to living intentionally is that making life changes can be intimidating. Goals such as focusing on the present, expressing creativity, or simply being happier can sound next to impossible when you don't even know where to begin. Making those big changes *is* possible, however, and the secret lies in starting small. To quote the ancient Chinese philosopher Lau Tzu, "A journey of a thousand miles must begin with a single step." Every change, no matter how momentous, starts with a single decision. Transforming that decision—the intent—into an action, something you can do today, is when change really begins.

That's where this journal comes in, providing a place for you to write down your daily intentions. Within these pages you'll find prompts that touch on various aspects of life, from physical well-being to life balance to emotional fulfillment. Guiding questions give you an opportunity to explore these topics and get in touch with your true intentions. Based on what you discover, you can then move on to figure out what changes you would like to make in your life, big or small.

To set daily intentions is to start your day awake. This journal is meant to help you focus in on what is truly important. Been feeling frustrated with a coworker? Perhaps setting the intention to give this person the benefit of the doubt and take a deep breath before reacting will help you live a more peaceful day. Been putting off doing the things that matter to you, like exercising or drawing? Setting the intention to clear time to focus on what makes you happy will lead to a more balanced life. Sometimes it's too easy for us to take the path of least resistance. With this journal, you're pledging to yourself to pay attention, to honor your hopes and goals, to become the person you want to be, and to live each day a little bit better.

Living with intention is not always easy. For that reason, it's important to keep this journal handy and revisit it often. Take time to read back over previous entries, both to reconnect with your intentions and to reassess how best to make a positive impact in the present moment. And it's ok to repeat intentions—after all, it requires focus to make lasting changes. Inspiring quotes scattered throughout are there to give you a daily boost and remind you that even history's greatest thinkers understood the importance of honoring your intentions. Meanwhile, if you get stuck thinking of intentions to set for yourself, the following list is full of examples that you can take directly or use as a springboard for creating your own.

As you work your way through this journal, setting intentions and meeting important goals, you'll undoubtedly sense a rise in self-confidence. That's the wonderful, natural result of taking charge of your life. Instead of resting on your laurels, though, make a commitment to harness that self-empowerment and use it to inspire change in others. Be warned: positive change is potent stuff! Once you decide to live a life of intent, there's no telling what you'll be able to accomplish.

INTENTIONS

If you're feeling stuck, here are some ideas of daily intentions to get you started.

Starting today, I will . . .

- GIVE PEOPLE THE BENEFIT OF THE DOUBT

- DO ONE TASK AT A TIME

- FORGIVE MY MISTAKES

- TAKE TIME TO APPRECIATE MY SURROUNDINGS

- ASK FOR HELP

- ❁ BELIEVE THAT I'M WORTH IT

- ❁ BE OPEN TO HAPPINESS

- ❁ DO SOMETHING FOR OTHERS

- ❁ BE PRESENT

- ❁ STOP AND BREATHE

- ❁ TRY SOMETHING NEW

- ❁ TRUST MY INSTINCTS

- ❁ ALLOW MYSELF TO DREAM BIG

- ❁ ASK QUESTIONS

- ❁ EXPRESS MYSELF

- ❁ BE MINDFUL OF MY ACTIONS

- ❁ LOVE OPENLY

- ❁ CHALLENGE MYSELF

- ❁ RECOGNIZE BAD HABITS

❀ BE CONSCIOUS OF MY FEELINGS

❀ BE POSITIVE

❀ LAUGH OUT LOUD

❀ BE THE CHANGE I WANT TO SEE IN
THE WORLD

❀ GET ORGANIZED

❀ REFUSE TO SETTLE

❀ FOLLOW MY OWN PATH

❀ FACE MY FEARS

❀ EXPLORE MY SURROUNDINGS

❀ CELEBRATE THE PEOPLE IN MY LIFE

❀ HOLD MYSELF ACCOUNTABLE

❀ AVOID SELF-PITY

❀ EMBRACE INDIVIDUALITY

- ✿ CREATE!
- ✿ INSPIRE POSITIVE CHANGE IN OTHERS
- ✿ LISTEN TO MY INNER VOICE
- ✿ BE GRATEFUL
- ✿ LEAVE THE PAST IN THE PAST
- ✿ TAKE CONTROL OF MY DESTINY
- ✿ LEARN FROM MY PAST MISTAKES
- ✿ BE HEALTHY
- ✿ KNOW MY LIMITS
- ✿ LEARN SOMETHING NEW
- ✿ SUPPORT MY COMMUNITY
- ✿ HAVE MORE FUN
- ✿ LISTEN TO OTHERS
- ✿ ONLY EXPECT THE BEST

- FORM MY OWN OPINIONS

- SMILE AS MUCH AS POSSIBLE

- SAY "I'M SORRY"

- BE SENSITIVE TO OTHERS' POINTS OF VIEW

Starting today, I will . . .

CREATE A LIST OF
ACTIVITIES THAT
MAKE YOU HAPPY.
Set the intention to do
one each week this
month. Write about how
this made you feel.

Starting today, I will . . .

Starting today, I will . . .

"WHAT YOU CAN DO, OR DREAM YOU CAN, BEGIN IT. BOLDNESS HAS GENIUS, POWER, AND MAGIC IN IT."

GOETHE

Starting today, I will . . .

Starting today, I will . . .

_____

_____

_____

_____

_____

_____

_____

THINK OF A TIME
WHEN YOU
FELT PROUD OF
SOMETHING YOU
ACCOMPLISHED.
How did you get there?
What can you focus
on today to bring you
closer to that feeling?

Starting today, I will . . .

Starting today, I will . . .

Starting today, I will . . .

Starting today, I will . . .

THINK OF THREE
PEOPLE YOU
ADMIRE, AND WRITE
ABOUT WHY.
What can you do today to
foster similar qualities?

Starting today, I will . . .

Starting today, I will . . .

Starting today, I will . . .

Starting today, I will . . .

MAKE A LIST OF
THE THINGS THAT
MAKE YOU ANGRIEST
DURING THE DAY.

Why do you think they
are so infuriating to you?
What can you intend to
do ahead of time to avoid
becoming upset, keeping
in mind that the answer
might be in how *you* deal
with a given situation?
Maybe the answer is as
simple as taking a breath
or going for a walk.

Starting today, I will . . .

Starting today, I will . . .

Starting today, I will . . .

Starting today, I will . . .

Starting today, I will . . .

Starting today, I will . . .

Starting today, I will . . .

PICK ONE PERSON
IN YOUR LIFE
WHO COULD USE
CHEERING UP.

Plan to do something

special this week to

lift their spirits, and then

write about what the

experience taught you

about your own life.

Starting today, I will . . .

Starting today, I will . . .

Starting today, I will . . .

"IT DOES NOT
MATTER HOW
SLOWLY YOU GO,
SO LONG AS
YOU DO NOT STOP."

CONFUCIUS

Starting today, I will . . .

Starting today, I will . . .

Starting today, I will . . .

WHAT ARE THREE
THINGS YOU WOULD
CHANGE ABOUT
YOUR LIFE TO MAKE
IT MORE FULFILLING?
What's holding you back?
What small things can
you do today to start
implementing these changes?

Starting today, I will . . .

Starting today, I will . . .

"CAUSE AND EFFECT,
MEANS AND ENDS, SEED
AND FRUIT CANNOT
BE SEVERED; FOR THE
EFFECT ALREADY BLOOMS
IN THE CAUSE, THE END
PREEXISTS IN THE MEANS,
THE FRUIT IN THE SEED."

RALPH WALDO EMERSON

Starting today, I will . . .

Starting today, I will . . .

Starting today, I will . . .

Starting today, I will . . .

Starting today, I will . . .

Starting today, I will . . .

THE BETTER WE SLEEP,
THE BETTER WE FEEL.
This week, intend to get a
great night of sleep every
night. Begin winding down
early and use relaxation
techniques, such as deep
breathing or visualization,
to ensure peaceful slumber.
Write about how your week
was improved.

Starting today, I will . . .

Starting today, I will . . .

Starting today, I will . . .

Starting today, I will . . .

Starting today, I will . . .

SPEND ONE DAY THIS
WEEK EXPLORING
A PLACE YOU'VE BEEN
MEANING TO VISIT
BUT HAVEN'T YET—
a local museum, art gallery,
or other cultural destination.
Write about your experience
and what specific things
inspired you. How did it feel
to finally go?

Starting today, I will . . .

Starting today, I will . . .

Starting today, I will . . .

Starting today, I will . . .

Starting today, I will . . .

Starting today, I will . . .

Starting today, I will . . .

WRITE ABOUT YOUR HIDDEN TALENTS AS WELL AS THE HIDDEN TALENTS THAT YOU *WISH* YOU HAD. Find one thing you can do today to nurture your talents, whether it's enrolling in a ceramics class or simply singing in the shower. Reflect on how this made you feel.

Starting today, I will . . .

Starting today, I will . . .

Starting today, I will . . .

Starting today, I will . . .

Starting today, I will . . .

_____

_____

_____

_____

_____

_____

DESCRIBE WHAT
AN AVERAGE DAY
WOULD BE LIKE
IN YOUR DREAM
CAREER.

What is one thing you
can do today to move
you closer to making that
dream a reality?

Starting today, I will . . .

Starting today, I will . . .

Starting today, I will . . .

"ONE CAN MAKE A
DAY OF ANY SIZE,
AND REGULATE THE
RISING AND SETTING
OF HIS OWN SUN
AND THE BRIGHTNESS
OF ITS SHINING."

JOHN MUIR

Starting today, I will . . .

Starting today, I will . . .

WHAT'S A
CONVERSATION THAT
YOU'VE BEEN
PUTTING OFF HAVING
BECAUSE OF HOW
YOU THOUGHT
THE PERSON MIGHT
REACT?

Pick a time this week to
start that conversation.
What other questions
have you been hesitant to
ask those around you?

Starting today, I will . . .

Starting today, I will . . .

Starting today, I will . . .

Starting today, I will . . .

Starting today, I will . . .

SMALL TURNS IN
THE ROAD CAN
SOMETIMES LEAD TO
BIG ADVENTURES.
Try altering something about
your daily routine each day
this week and see what new
paths open up for you.

Starting today, I will . . .

Starting today, I will . . .

"LIFE IS EITHER A DARING ADVENTURE OR NOTHING. TO KEEP OUR FACES TOWARD CHANGE AND BEHAVE LIKE FREE SPIRITS IN THE PRESENCE OF FATE IS STRENGTH UNDEFEATABLE."

HELEN KELLER

Starting today, I will . . .

Starting today, I will . . .

Starting today, I will . . .

Starting today, I will . . .

SPEND AN HOUR
OR TWO THIS WEEK
CREATING A
VISION COLLAGE:
use cutout images from
magazines, blogs, and
elsewhere that project
an image of how you see
your ideal life and the
person you wish to be.
What insight can you glean?

Starting today, I will . . .

Starting today, I will . . .

Starting today, I will . . .

Starting today, I will . . .

Starting today, I will . . .

Starting today, I will . . .

_____

_____

_____

_____

_____

_____

_____

_____

THINK OF A TIME
WHEN SOMEONE—
a friend, parent, teacher,
or other role model—
inspired a positive change
in you. What can you do
today to inspire a positive
change in someone else?

Starting today, I will . . .

Starting today, I will . . .

Starting today, I will . . .

Starting today, I will . . .

Starting today, I will . . .

WHAT DID YOU
WANT TO BE WHEN
YOU GREW UP?

Are you doing it? If not,
what changed along the way?
This week, think about
how you can incorporate
those early aspirations into
your current life.

Starting today, I will . . .

"DO WHAT YOU CAN, WITH WHAT YOU HAVE, WHERE YOU ARE."

THEODORE ROOSEVELT

Starting today, I will . . .

Starting today, I will . . .

Starting today, I will . . .

_____

_____

_____

_____

_____

_____

_____

_____

_____

> MAKE A PROS AND
> CONS LIST ABOUT
> YOUR CURRENT JOB.
> What conclusions can
> you draw? What are some
> cons that you can focus
> on changing today?

_____

_____

_____

_____

_____

_____

_____

_____

Starting today, I will . . .

Starting today, I will . . .

Starting today, I will . . .

Starting today, I will . . .

Starting today, I will . . .

Starting today, I will . . .

THINK ABOUT WHAT
IT MEANS TO BE
A GOOD FRIEND.

Create a friend report card
for yourself, assessing how
good of a friend you think
you have been. In which
areas do you excel? Which
could use improvement?

Starting today, I will . . .

Starting today, I will . . .

Starting today, I will . . .

Starting today, I will . . .

Starting today, I will . . .

_____

_____

_____

_____

_____

_____

_____

_____

_____

_____

_____

_____

THIS WEEK, PUT
YOUR ENERGY INTO
LEARNING HOW
TO DO SOMETHING
that you've always been
interested in, like learning
to sew or even whistling.
Imagine what other things
you could learn to do if you
made the time.

Starting today, I will . . .

Starting today, I will . . .

Starting today, I will . . .

Starting today, I will . . .

"NOT EVERYTHING THAT IS FACED CAN BE CHANGED UNTIL IT IS FACED."

JAMES BALDWIN

Starting today, I will . . .

Starting today, I will . . .

Starting today, I will . . .

Starting today, I will . . .

Starting today, I will . . .

TODAY, FOCUS
ON NOT JUST
HEARING OTHER
PEOPLE BUT TRULY
LISTENING TO THEM.
What sort of things did
you learn that you might
otherwise not have?

Starting today, I will . . .

Starting today, I will . . .

"SUCCESS OFTEN COMES TO THOSE WHO DARE AND ACT; IT SELDOM GOES TO THE TIMID WHO ARE EVER AFRAID OF THE CONSEQUENCES."

JAWAHARLAL NEHRU

Starting today, I will . . .

Starting today, I will . . .

SET UP AN INTERVIEW
THIS WEEK WITH
SOMEONE WHO
YOU FEEL IS LIVING
THEIR DREAM.

What sorts of questions
would you like to ask them?
What lessons from their
life can you use in your own?

Starting today, I will . . .

Starting today, I will . . .

Starting today, I will . . .

Starting today, I will . . .

Starting today, I will . . .

Starting today, I will . . .

THEY SAY THAT
LAUGHTER IS THE
BEST MEDICINE.
Today, find as many excuses
as possible to laugh, and see
how your mood improves.

Starting today, I will . . .

Starting today, I will . . .

Starting today, I will . . .

Starting today, I will . . .

Starting today, I will . . .

Starting today, I will . . .

WHAT ARE THREE
THINGS YOU WOULD
CHANGE ABOUT
YOUR LIFE TO MAKE
IT MORE FULFILLING?

What's holding you back?

What small things can

you do today to start

implementing these changes?

Starting today, I will . . .

Starting today, I will . . .

Starting today, I will . . .

Starting today, I will . . .

Starting today, I will . . .

MAKE A LIST OF
QUIET SPOTS, EITHER
NEAR YOUR
HOME OR WORK.
Visit one of these spots
each day this week and
spend at least fifteen
minutes enjoying the silence
and reflecting on your life.

Starting today, I will . . .

Starting today, I will . . .

Starting today, I will . . .

Starting today, I will . . .

Starting today, I will . . .

Starting today, I will . . .

Starting today, I will . . .

SET YOUR
INTENTION TO SAY
THANK YOU TO
AS MANY PEOPLE AS
POSSIBLE TODAY,
and then write about how
they responded and
how it made you feel. What
did this teach
you about your daily life?

Starting today, I will . . .

Starting today, I will . . .

Starting today, I will . . .

Starting today, I will . . .

"LIFE IS NOT LONG,
AND TOO MUCH OF IT
MUST NOT PASS
IN IDLE DELIBERATION
OF HOW IT SHALL
BE SPENT."

SAMUEL JOHNSON

Starting today, I will . . .

Starting today, I will . . .

Starting today, I will . . .

Starting today, I will . . .

Starting today, I will . . .

Starting today, I will . . .

WRITE ABOUT A TIME
WHEN SOMEONE
MADE YOU FEEL
TRULY APPRECIATED.
How did that feel? Have
you been meaning to
acknowledge someone?
What are some opportunities
for you to show appreciation
for someone else today?

"THERE'S ONLY ONE CORNER OF THE UNIVERSE YOU CAN BE CERTAIN OF IMPROVING, AND THAT IS YOUR OWN SELF."

ALDOUS HUXLEY

Starting today, I will . . .

Starting today, I will . . .

Starting today, I will . . .

Starting today, I will . . .

DESCRIBE A
RELATIONSHIP—
EITHER ONE OF
YOURS OR
A FRIEND'S—
that you consider to be
healthy. What are its
defining characteristics?
What is something you
can do today to foster
those same characteristics
in all your relationships?

Starting today, I will . . .

Starting today, I will . . .

Starting today, I will . . .

DATE

Starting today, I will . . .

Starting today, I will . . .

Starting today, I will . . .

Starting today, I will . . .

TAKE A FEW MINUTES
TO WRITE DOWN WHY
YOU'VE DECIDED TO
KEEP THIS JOURNAL.

What are you hoping to
accomplish? What are your
personal intentions for it?
Throughout the year, keep
flipping back to this page to
keep yourself on track.

Starting today, I will . . .

Starting today, I will . . .

Starting today, I will . . .

Starting today, I will . . .

Starting today, I will . . .

MAKE A LIST OF THE
THINGS YOU'VE BEEN
MEANING TO FIX.

Maybe it's a rusty bike,
a chipped vase, or a broken
picture frame. Set your
intention to either fix one
thing or finally get it into the
trash and out of mind.

Starting today, I will . . .

Starting today, I will . . .

Starting today, I will . . .

Starting today, I will . . .

Starting today, I will . . .

PICK A DAY THIS
WEEK TO ASK FOR
FEEDBACK FROM ONE
OF YOUR FRIENDS
ON HOW THEY VIEW
YOUR LIFE.

How does their impression

differ from yours? Does

their feedback inspire you

to make any changes,

either in how you live or how

you see yourself?

Starting today, I will . . .

Starting today, I will . . .

Starting today, I will . . .

Starting today, I will . . .

_____

_____

_____

_____

_____

_____

_____

_____

_____

_____

_____

_____

_____

ORGANIZING YOUR
LIFE IS A BIG JOB,
BUT YOU CAN MAKE
IT MANAGEABLE BY
STARTING SMALL.
This week pick one area of
your life, whether
it's your closet or your taxes,
to organize. What further
steps can you take to make
organization a part of
your daily routine?

Starting today, I will . . .

Starting today, I will . . .

Starting today, I will . . .

"NOTHING EVER BECOMES REAL TILL IT IS EXPERIENCED."

JOHN KEATS

Starting today, I will . . .

Starting today, I will . . .

Starting today, I will . . .

THINK ABOUT THE
BIG DECISIONS
IN YOUR LIFE THAT
BROUGHT YOU
TO THE PLACE YOU
ARE NOW.

What different choices
would you have made in
retrospect? How can you
apply those lessons to a
decision you're facing in
your life today?

Starting today, I will . . .

Starting today, I will . . .

"FOREVER—
IS COMPOSED
OF NOWS."

EMILY DICKINSON

Starting today, I will . . .

Starting today, I will . . .

Starting today, I will . . .

Starting today, I will . . .

Starting today, I will . . .

Starting today, I will . . .

THROUGHOUT
TODAY, SAY HELLO
TO AS MANY PEOPLE
AS POSSIBLE—
EVEN STRANGERS.
What sort of interactions
took place? What did this
teach you about your life?

Starting today, I will . . .

Starting today, I will . . .

Starting today, I will . . .

TODAY, CONCENTRATE ON RECOGNIZING AS MANY NEGATIVE THOUGHTS AS POSSIBLE AND REPLACING THEM WITH POSITIVE THOUGHTS.

How successful were you? What are other ways of promoting positivity?

Starting today, I will . . .

Starting today, I will . . .

Starting today, I will . . .

Starting today, I will . . .

Starting today, I will . . .

Starting today, I will . . .

Starting today, I will . . .

THINK BIG!
PICK A PROJECT
THAT YOU'VE BEEN
HESITANT TO START
BECAUSE IT SIMPLY
FEELS TOO BIG.
Today, spend thirty minutes
setting your project in
motion, whether that means
making a list of supplies or
doing online research.

"THE LIVING MOMENT IS EVERYTHING."

D. H. LAWRENCE

Starting today, I will . . .

Starting today, I will . . .

Starting today, I will . . .

Starting today, I will . . .

TODAY, FOCUS
ON NOT JUST
HEARING OTHER
PEOPLE BUT TRULY
LISTENING TO THEM.
What sort of things did
you learn that you might
otherwise not have?

DATE

Starting today, I will . . .

Starting today, I will . . .

Starting today, I will . . .

Starting today, I will . . .

Starting today, I will . . .

Starting today, I will . . .

"MAY YOU LIVE ALL THE DAYS OF YOUR LIFE."

JONATHAN SWIFT

Starting today, I will . . .

THINK ABOUT A
TIME WHEN SOMEONE
FORGAVE YOU.
What were the circumstances
and how did the experience
make you feel? Is there
anything that you need to
forgive *yourself* for today?

Starting today, I will . . .

Starting today, I will . . .

Starting today, I will . . .

"GREAT THINGS
ARE NOT DONE BY
IMPULSE, BUT BY A
SERIES OF SMALL
THINGS BROUGHT
TOGETHER."

VINCENT VAN GOGH

Starting today, I will . . .

Starting today, I will . . .

INTEND TO WAKE UP
ONE HOUR EARLY
EACH DAY THIS WEEK,
and spend the extra time
doing something you enjoy.
At the end of the week, write
about what the extra time
allowed you to accomplish.

Starting today, I will . . .

Starting today, I will . . .

Starting today, I will . . .

Starting today, I will . . .

Starting today, I will . . .

WHAT ARE THREE
THINGS YOU
WOULD CHANGE
ABOUT YOUR LIFE
to make it more fulfilling?
What's holding you
back? What small things
can you do today to
start implementing
these changes?

Starting today, I will . . .

Starting today, I will . . .

Starting today, I will . . .

Starting today, I will . . .

Starting today, I will . . .

OUTLINE YOUR
OVERALL
HEALTH GOALS.

What are the biggest
obstacles to achieving those
goals? What is one
thing you could do each
day—related to exercise
or diet, for instance—
that will bring you closer
to your goal?

Starting today, I will . . .

Starting today, I will . . .

Starting today, I will . . .

Starting today, I will . . .

Starting today, I will . . .

"THEY ALWAYS SAY THAT TIME CHANGES THINGS, BUT YOU ACTUALLY HAVE TO CHANGE THEM YOURSELF."

ANDY WARHOL

Starting today, I will . . .

Starting today, I will . . .

WHICH TIMES
DURING THE DAY
ARE THE MOST
STRESSFUL?

What are the circumstances
surrounding those times?
Today, choose an affirming
phrase, such as "I am perfect
just how I am," and repeat
it to yourself whenever you
feel overcome by stress.

Starting today, I will . . .

Starting today, I will . . .

Starting today, I will . . .

Starting today, I will . . .

Starting today, I will . . .

Starting today, I will . . .

Starting today, I will . . .

Starting today, I will . . .

Starting today, I will . . .

MAKE A LIST OF
EVENTS OR ACTIVITIES
THAT YOU'VE BEEN
LONGING TO DO.
This week, take yourself on
a date and treat yourself to
one of those activities. How
did this make you feel? Plan
to do it next week, too!

Starting today, I will . . .

Starting today, I will . . .

Starting today, I will . . .

MAKE A LIST OF ALL
THE THINGS YOU ARE
GRATEFUL FOR
(it's okay if you go through
several pages!). Think of
ways that you can express
your gratitude this week.

Starting today, I will . . .

Starting today, I will . . .

"DESTINY IS NOT A MATTER OF CHANCE, IT IS A MATTER OF CHOICE. IT IS NOT A THING TO BE WAITED FOR; IT IS A THING TO BE ACHIEVED."

WILLIAM JENNINGS BRYAN

Starting today, I will . . .

Starting today, I will . . .

Starting today, I will . . .

Starting today, I will . . .

Starting today, I will . . .

THIS WEEK, RESEARCH
LOCAL GROUPS THAT
SOUND INTERESTING
TO YOU—
a cooking club, a book group,
or something more
adventurous. What do you
think you could gain from
joining? What's holding
you back?

Starting today, I will . . .

Starting today, I will . . .

Starting today, I will . . .

"THE VALUE OF
ACHIEVEMENT
LIES IN THE
ACHIEVING."

ALBERT EINSTEIN

Starting today, I will . . .

Starting today, I will . . .

Starting today, I will . . .

WRITE ABOUT THE
ONE THING THAT
MADE YOU
HAPPIEST AS A CHILD.
How can you reconnect with
that happiness today?

Starting today, I will . . .

Starting today, I will . . .

Starting today, I will . . .

Starting today, I will . . .

Starting today, I will . . .

Starting today, I will . . .

Starting today, I will . . .

Starting today, I will . . .

Starting today, I will . . .

WRITE ABOUT WHERE
YOU WOULD LIKE
TO BE IN FIVE YEARS.

Which parts of your life
would be different? Which
would stay the same? What
are some practical things
you can do today to help you
reach your goals?

Starting today, I will . . .

Starting today, I will . . .

Starting today, I will . . .

Starting today, I will . . .

Starting today, I will . . .

Starting today, I will . . .

WHAT ARE THREE
THINGS YOU WOULD
CHANGE ABOUT
THE WORLD TO MAKE
IT A BETTER PLACE?
How can you help enact
those changes today?

Starting today, I will . . .

Starting today, I will . . .

Starting today, I will . . .

Starting today, I will . . .

Starting today, I will . . .

THINK OF AN OLD
FRIEND YOU'VE LOST
TOUCH WITH.

What has changed in your
life since last you spoke?
How do you feel about where
you are now? Today, reach
out and make contact.

"I SAY THAT THE STRONGEST PRINCIPLE OF GROWTH LIES IN HUMAN CHOICE."

GEORGE ELIOT

Starting today, I will . . .

Starting today, I will . . .

Starting today, I will . . .

_____

_____

_____

_____

_____

_____

_____

_____

_____

_____

_____

_____

_____

_____

_____

_____

_____

_____

_____

_____

"YESTERDAY IS GONE; TOMORROW HAS NOT YET COME. WE HAVE ONLY TODAY. LET US BEGIN."

MOTHER TERESA

Starting today, I will . . .

Starting today, I will . . .

Starting today, I will . . .

Starting today, I will . . .

Starting today, I will . . .

Starting today, I will . . .

"WELL DONE
IS BETTER THAN
WELL SAID."

Starting today, I will . . .

WHAT ARE THREE
THINGS YOU
WOULD CHANGE
ABOUT YOUR LIFE
to make it more fulfilling?
What's holding you
back? What small things
can you do today to
start implementing
these changes?

Starting today, I will . . .

"IT IS HARD TO FAIL, BUT IT IS WORSE NEVER TO HAVE TRIED TO SUCCEED."

THEODORE ROOSEVELT

Starting today, I will . . .

Starting today, I will . . .

Starting today, I will . . .

Starting today, I will . . .

Starting today, I will . . .

Starting today, I will . . .

Starting today, I will . . .

WRITE A LETTER
TO YOUR
YOUNGER SELF,
explaining who you've
become and how you
got there. What parts of
the letter made you feel
good? Which parts, if
any, felt disappointing?

Starting today, I will . . .

Starting today, I will . . .

Starting today, I will . . .

WRITE ABOUT THE
LAST TIME YOU DID
SOMETHING THAT
REALLY MADE YOU
FEEL ALIVE.

This week, dare yourself to
do something that takes you
out of your comfort zone,
like participating in an
open mic night or signing up
for skydiving lessons.

Starting today, I will . . .

Starting today, I will . . .

Starting today, I will . . .

Starting today, I will . . .

Starting today, I will . . .

Starting today, I will . . .

Starting today, I will . . .

_____

_____

_____

_____

_____

_____

_____

_____

_____

_____

_____

_____

_____

_____

_____

_____

MAKE A LIST OF
YOUR BAD HABITS.
How did they start and what
might be their underlying
causes? Make a point today
of refraining from one bad
habit, and write about how
it made a difference in your
day. Outline a plan of how
you can continue forming
better habits.

Starting today, I will . . .

"CHANGE YOUR LIFE TODAY. DON'T GAMBLE ON THE FUTURE; ACT NOW, WITHOUT DELAY."

SIMONE DE BEAUVOIR

Starting today, I will . . .

Starting today, I will . . .

Starting today, I will . . .

Starting today, I will . . .

Starting today, I will . . .

Starting today, I will . . .

Starting today, I will . . .

VISIT THE LIBRARY
AND PICK OUT A
BIOGRAPHY OF
SOMEONE WHO
INSPIRES YOU.

How did that person deal
with issues similar to those
you face? What insight
can you apply to your own
life today?

Starting today, I will . . .

Starting today, I will . . .

Starting today, I will . . .

Starting today, I will . . .

HOW DOES
YOUR OUTWARD
APPEARANCE
AFFECT THE WAY YOU
SEE YOURSELF?

Looking our best helps
us feel our best, too. Today,
do one thing that helps
you better represent your
true self, like cleaning out
your closet, exercising, or
scheduling an overdue haircut.

Starting today, I will . . .

Starting today, I will . . .

Starting today, I will . . .

Starting today, I will . . .

Starting today, I will . . .

Starting today, I will . . .

Starting today, I will . . .

TODAY, CONCENTRATE ON RECOGNIZING AS MANY NEGATIVE THOUGHTS AS POSSIBLE AND REPLACING THEM WITH POSITIVE THOUGHTS.

How successful were you? What are other ways of promoting positivity?

Starting today, I will . . .

Starting today, I will . . .

Starting today, I will . . .

Starting today, I will . . .

"LET US NOT LOOK BACK IN ANGER, NOR FORWARD IN FEAR, BUT AROUND IN AWARENESS."

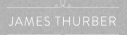

JAMES THURBER

Starting today, I will . . .

Starting today, I will . . .

_____

_____

_____

_____

_____

_____

_____

WRITE ABOUT A
TIME WHEN YOU
SUCCESSFULLY FACED
YOUR FEARS.

How did you go about it?
What similar techniques
could you use to overcome
fear today?

_____

_____

_____

_____

_____

_____

_____

_____

Starting today, I will . . .

Starting today, I will . . .

Starting today, I will . . .

"WHY ALWAYS 'NOT YET'? DO FLOWERS IN SPRING SAY 'NOT YET'?"

NORMAN DOUGLAS

Starting today, I will . . .

Starting today, I will . . .

Starting today, I will . . .

Starting today, I will . . .

Starting today, I will . . .

Starting today, I will . . .

Starting today, I will . . .

Starting today, I will . . .

Starting today, I will . . .

Starting today, I will . . .

_____

_____

_____

_____

_____

_____

WHAT ARE THREE
THINGS YOU WOULD
CHANGE ABOUT
YOUR LIFE TO MAKE
IT MORE FULFILLING?
What's holding you back?
What small things can
you do today to start
implementing these changes?

Starting today, I will . . .

Starting today, I will . . .

Starting today, I will . . .

Starting today, I will . . .

Starting today, I will . . .

Starting today, I will . . .

Starting today, I will . . .

> THINK ABOUT A TIME
> WHEN YOU GAVE
> YOUR TRUST
> OVER TO SOMEONE.
> What were the
> circumstances and the
> outcome? Today,
> find ways to instill trust
> in others and have them
> put their trust in you.

Starting today, I will . . .

"THE BITTEREST TEARS SHED OVER GRAVES ARE FOR WORDS LEFT UNSAID AND DEEDS LEFT UNDONE."

HARRIET BEECHER STOWE

Starting today, I will . . .